Business Planning Made Simple

Creating A Strategic Guide For Your Success Journey

Business Planning

Planning

Made Simple

Creating A

Strategic Guide

For Your

Success Journey

Steve Hoffacker

AICP, CAASH, CAPS, CGA, CGP, CMP, CSP, MCSP, MIRM

Business Planning

Made Simple

Creating A Strategic Guide For Your Success Journey

Cover photo by Steve Hoffacker.

ALL RIGHTS RESERVED.

———

This book is dedicated to the success of anyone in sales or business — whether just starting out or a veteran of years of business experience — that needs a plan for their success. This includes onsite new home salespeople, small volume and custom home builders, real estate sales professionals, real estate brokers, sales managers of any type business, marketing managers, small business owners, shopkeepers, professionals, network marketers, home-based businesses, online businesses, B2B sales, B2C sales, contractors, remodelers, consultants, and anyone else who earns their living by selling.

———

Books, Articles, Blogs & Other Sales Content By Steve Hoffacker

To access or learn about books, eBooks, articles, blogs, commentary, podcasts, videos, webinars, and other content by Steve Hoffacker for anyone who sells products or services for a living, use the sites below.

"Hoffacker Associates" Website
http://stevehoffacker.com

Steve Hoffacker's Amazon.com Author Page
http://amazon.com/author/stevehoffacker

"Steve Hoffacker's Home Sales Insights" Blog
http://homesalesinsights.com

"Steve Hoffacker's Sales Quips" Blog
http://salesquips.com

"Steve Hoffacker's Success Quips" Blog
http://successquips.com

Steve Hoffacker and Hoffacker Associates can be found online at Facebook, Active Rain, Pinterest, Linked-In, Plaxo, Twitter, Goggle+, YouTube, Tumblr, and other business, real estate, and social sites.

Table Of Contents

Preface

I wrote this book as an extension of the material that I teach as part of a business management class required for the Certified Aging-in-Place Specialist (CAPS) designation that the National Association of Home Builders (NAHB) offers.

The coursework touches on some of these aspects, but I wanted to expand upon them, and the book you now have is a result of those efforts.

I first prepared and published this book as an Amazon Kindle eBook to get the material released and out to business owners and entrepreneurs quicker than would have been the case with a published, formatted book.

Now that I have completed the text you are holding, you (and other readers) have your choice of accessing and reading a digital format on your portable device or PC (although it looks somewhat different from the printed version) or holding and reading a traditional trade paperback — or you can get both of them.

The two versions are essentially the same, but the print edition is larger because there are many places and opportunities for you to record your thoughts directly in the text (using it like a workbook or journal) that are not possible in the digital edition.

There just is no way for you to record your ideas directly onto the digital version. You will need to keep a pad with you as you read so you can make notes.

The reason this book is important for you to read and use is that most small businesses or commissioned salespeople operate in the moment without any type of long-term plan other than perhaps a mental picture of what they would like to do.

If you already have completed a formal written plan, you have done something that few small businesses do.

Nevertheless, I encourage you to compare what you have now with the questions I pose to you in this text to see if there are any areas of your plan that you may want to revise, bolster, reconsider, or supplement.

It's not that people have no plan. They generally have some idea in their mind — however rough or basic it might be — of a direction, mission, sales volume, or total revenue/income they would like to achieve, but they haven't dotted all of the "i's" and crossed the "t's."

Until they sit down to actually put something in writing, people generally don't think through where they are going and what they will need to get there.

It's much more than just showing up to work every day or doing something that you enjoy. There has to be a framework or purpose in which you do your business, and it has to make sense to you.

To help you get to the point that you are making effective decisions and delivering your products or services in the optimal way, you need to examine the major components of your business and make sure that you have planned for what you want and that you are doing what you planned.

There are many reasons why people who don't have a written plan have never completed one. We will look at some of those reasons as we go along. Some people have likely never given a written plan any serious thought — regardless of what goes into creating one.

One of the chief concerns for a business without a written plan — whether there a few people involved in the business or just the business owner as a sole practitioner — is that no one has any idea of what the aims of the business are and how to go about accomplishing them except the person with the mental plan.

As such, no one (family, friends, strategic partners, associates, or employees) can help that person achieve their mission or get the business back on track after an illness, injury, or market slowdown because no one can pick up anything to read about how the business is structured or run. The plan would have to be communicated from the business owner in the best way possible to those who want to help.

Without the thought process that goes into preparing a written plan, the business owner may have difficulty organizing and conveying his or her ideas of what needs to happen to move the business forward.

There seems to be general confusion over just what a written business plan needs to do or accomplish and what it should look like if and when it is attempted.

Often, when we hear someone speak of a written business plan, we think that it must be a fairly large document and include a lot of financial details for lenders or potential investors to use as they consider the merits of helping to fund the business.

There certainly are those types of business plans, but there also are written plans that are used to crystallize the thinking and direction of a company and to guide its daily actions.

It's this second type of plan that we are looking at in this book — the type that any business can and should create to have a guide for steering the business and the decisions that have to be made about market area, staffing, strategic relationships, managing resources, acquiring new business, servicing accounts, adding or eliminating products and services, vendor relationships, marketing, sales, management, order fulfillment, and more.

The business plan begins with an assessment of what the company or sales operation is all about. There must be a purpose, a vision, and a mission.

Then other elements are added to guide your decisions and serve as a blueprint for your business success.

Whether you are a commissioned salesperson working for another organization (where it essentially is your business) or this is your own business (with or without employees), you need to determine your vision and mission, translate those concepts into objectives, set goals to reach those objectives, and then work your plan to achieve the success you seek.

It doesn't matter at this point if this is a business that you have been involved with for several months or years or if it's something that you're just preparing to launch.

Planning will serve you no matter where you are in your company's history and journey.

When you begin thinking about the questions that I ask you to consider in this book concerning your business and where you want it to head — and then answer them at your own pace and on your schedule — you will be developing a strong game plan to map your success.

Again, this text has not been prepared to help you create a prospectus or vehicle for soliciting financial contributors or investors although it may serve you well in doing that.

Rather, it's designed strictly to give you the tools to use to create a written framework for your business to allow you to manage your plan and guide your performance, growth, revenues, profitability, and success.

A written plan such as you will be able to create with the help from this text is so often missing in business.

No one else can write a plan for your business the way that you can. No one else has the commitment to your business or to your aspect of the business (such as the sales function) that you do.

You need to know how well you are doing toward staying on target and true to your plan. With that in mind, let's get started.

Business Planning Made Simple

Creating A
Strategic Guide
For Your
Success Journey

1

Why Should You Plan?

Businesses Have Various Launch Schedules

Not all businesses are created equal in terms of how they are launched.

If you were employed somewhere else at the time you started your business and had an income stream that was not dependent on the success of your new venture, you could have taken your time in launching it.

You might have worked on the idea for months before ever opening your doors or going public with your business.

If you currently are just in the "thinking-about-it" stage of starting a new business and are still working for someone else or have a source of income, you can take some time in getting your new business organized and started. There is no particular pressure to open by a certain date other than personal preference.

Some people are forced into either finding a new job or starting a business when their source of income drastically and immediately changes.

They decided to launch a new business quickly without the luxury of weeks or months of getting ready because what they were doing suddenly stopped being a source of income for them.

They decided to open their business when they were discharged, forced out, had the company go out of business, or had other market factors that made continuing with their employment impractical.

Some people launch businesses fresh out of college or military service and have never held a permanent job working for someone else.

Some start out in the family business and eventually take over managing, running, or owning it — on their own or with other family members.

Some people are doing commissioned sales — meaning that they don't legally own the business, product, or service they represent — but they function as if it is their business as they make decisions on developing sales leads, marketing, promotion, sustainability, sales, and repeat business just like their name was on the door.

In every real sense, having a sales business without a guaranteed income is just like being in business and running it.

Thus, there are many timetables for getting started in business.

Some people have more time than others for getting ready, planning, and assimilating into being on their own.

Business Planning Isn't A Requirement

If you took your time in getting your business ready to launch, you quite likely engaged in hours of planning.

Maybe your wrote out a plan; maybe you just considered many possible directions and ideas without actually writing them down. You certainly devoted many hours to thinking about your new business.

Perhaps you wrote a very basic plan; maybe you just jotted down some notes. Possibly you just kept mental notes and ideas.

You could be at that pre-launch stage right now where you are collecting your thoughts, looking for more direction, and trying to create a plan of success before you officially launch your business.

If you work for a large organization, you might have had a sales territory given to you and thrust into making a go of it without much direction other than product knowledge and your sales skills.

Starting a successful business takes many skills and attributes.

Planning for your success is desirable, but it is not a requirement (if you truly are in business for yourself).

Nothing says that you have to have a business plan, a sense of direction, specific goals, objectives, a vision, a formal mission statement, a business checking account, organizational ability, systems in place (accounting, billing, bidding, warranty), employees, advertising, or other aspects often associated with beginning or running a business.

Essentially, you need drive, enthusiasm, and knowledge of how to do what you are offering.

The rest you can pick up as you go.

Of course, the more have going into your venture, the more you can concentrate on growing your business rather than learning how to be in business.

Because having a written business plan is not something that anyone requires to open or run a business (unless you are seeking funding or financial backers or you run a sales operation for another company), many businesses have never had one.

Business Planning Doesn't Require An MBA

Business planning is one of those concepts that sounds like it's best left to the MBAs and should not be touched by the average business owner or salesperson.

It sounds like we need special training in finance, management, personnel, and other business elements in order to pull it off successfully.

Nevertheless, it is essentially a very simple process to do once the thinking and evaluation parts are completed.

It's something we all can do — right where we are without any additional training (other than using some of the guidelines that are found here in this text).

Unless you are preparing a plan to solicit capital for your start-up business or for business expansion, writing a business plan does not have to be so formal, rigid, or daunting. Also, it doesn't need to include a pro forma or budgets. You can add those elements or use them in your plan, but they aren't required.

All your written business plan needs to do is answer the questions you pose to yourself about the nature, purpose, function, and direction of your business and then serve as a constant guide to keep you headed on the right path.

It's A Tool For You

You want to address the important aspects of your business in creating your plan, but your focus is in doing it as a roadmap for your success and not as a prospectus for investors.

For our discussions here, we are interested in your success — immediate as well as long-term.

Therefore, the business planning we are talking about is designed to help you succeed in your particular business or sales function by identifying the essential parts of your business and evaluating and optimizing their relationships with each other.

The reason you should want to spend the time required to produce a written business plan is not because potential funding depends on it (although you may choose do this later) but because (1) it makes you focus on, think of, and actually write down what you want to accomplish, and (2) it provides an actual strategy or roadmap for getting there — as well as providing a timetable for critical benchmarks.

Just like any other important resource you use in your business, your written business plan — when you complete it — will be a management tool to guide your business decisions, direction, and pace.

Choosing The Best Route

I'm sure you've heard that failing to plan is planning to fail.

That's a little simplistic for our purposes because hardly anyone approaches their business with no plan whatsoever. However casual or undefined it is, nearly everyone has some idea where they want to go or what they would like to accomplish.

Nevertheless, with an undefined or fluid plan that is not written down but only kept as a mental image, things can change from day-to-day or job-to-job.

This impacts the work you think about or decide to bid on or pursue, the direction you want to go, your level of confidence in approaching a particular assignment or project, strategic relationships you decide to form, geographic and demographic markets you pursue, and what both you and the marketplace think you are by the way you package and market yourself.

The challenge in running your business or enterprise effectively is having the ability to be true to yourself and what you offer — to be efficient and productive at doing what you're the best at providing.

Thus, a long range plan that is carefully thought out and then written down will do more for your success than just a rough idea of what you want to accomplish each day — and not being totally sure of how it fits into a larger goal or objective.

Just letting things happen and then responding to them is not an effective way to conduct your business. There is no continuity of effort or direction.

You want your efforts and the time that you are investing in running your business to work in harmony. You want one action to complement another.

You want to select a path to follow that will focus your energies rather than scattering or diffusing them.

Focusing Your Energies

In short, the reason that you should take the time to plan and then write it down is to focus your energies on accomplishing that which you have determined you want to achieve.

The planning process itself is powerful. Then the finished plan keeps you on target as an official document summarizing all of your planning.

This focus and concentration on what you want to achieve, the resources that you will need, and how you are going to accomplish your plan allows you to involve your subconscience, your senses, and your trusted associates in helping you to succeed.

It lets you make decisions about potential business to go after or accept, people to involve in your business, customers to pursue or accept, equipment or property to acquire or consider, and other very important aspects of running a successful business.

It will keep you from wasting time, energy, and money in pursuing avenues that sound attractive but don't align with your plan.

Along the way, you may determine that you need the efforts and support of your family, close friends, staff, associates, virtual assistants, trade contractors, professional services firms, and strategic partners to keep you on track and to accomplish what you have set out to do.

This is quite sound and very strategic.

When you have a written plan that you have shared with a close circle of advisors, they can help you be accountable to your plan.

They can watch out for you and help your plan succeed.

The Journalistic Approach

Writing your personal business plan is much like writing a good story.

You might recall from your days in journalism or English class, or perhaps on the school paper, that you need to address the central questions of who, what, when, where, how, why, and which in composing a story.

Writing your business plan is quite similar in this regard.

However, there may be some overlap between various components of your plan and you don't need to address the central questions in any certain order.

After all, this is your plan. You may choose to share it or have it reviewed by a close circle of trusted advisors (I'll address this more later), but it is still your plan that doesn't need to receive or win the approval of anyone else.

I gave you a few blank lines here in this section where you can make some preliminary notes as ideas come to you. There is a more expansive section coming up in Chapter 3 where you will make more extensive notes.

Start with "who." Look at and then determine who you are as a business, who helps you acquire new business, who helps you produce and fulfill your orders, who can rely on to help you build your business right now, who you might need as a resource going forward to help you, and who you intend to serve.

_____
_____
_____
_____
_____

Your competition is a large "who" that you need to identify and prepare to address — who else is targeting or appealing to the market that you intend to serve.

_____
_____
_____
_____
_____

Then look at "what." You'll decide or identify what it is that you do well and what it is that you want to continue doing or change — as well as what you have and what you'll need in terms of resources to help you be more successful.

_____
_____
_____
_____
_____

Look at what specifically you offer the marketplace and if that is profitable, viable, and effective.

_____

_____

_____

_____

Identify what you want to use to promote yourself and the physical requirements of running your business (office, equipment, personnel, vehicles, uniforms, paperwork, software, and tools, for instance).

_____

_____

_____

_____

Look at "when" you want to complete your plan as well as when the plan begins — whether that's in stages or in its entirety, from months to several years — and establish interim checkpoints for assessing your progress and keep you on track.

If you haven't formally begun your business yet, you'll want to determine when you are actually going to begin.

_____

_____

_____

_____

_____

For "where," look at where your business is centered now — both in terms of your office or location and the market, markets, population, or demographics you serve — and determine if you like where you are and if, when, and how you might want that to change.

_____

_____

_____

_____

_____

_____

"How" do you intend to market your business, make sales, fulfill orders, generate revenue, manage cash flow, add or remove products or services, address technological advances, gain a larger market share, retain your customers and make repeat sales, warranty your work, determine your effectiveness, and generally be a success?

_____

_____

_____

_____

_____

_____

Reveal "why" you started your business or joined the organization you're with and what keeps you going.

_____

_____

_____

_____

_____

Decide "which" markets, products, price points, and opportunities to pursue — and which areas of your business you may want to expand or adjust.

_____

_____

_____

_____

_____

_____

Then, you'll put all of your ideas in writing and get started on your success journey.

However, there are more questions to consider and answer first.

2

Planning Is Not A High Priority

Often It's Not A Conscious Decision

Probably more people in business or independent sales than not would agree that having a written business plan is a good idea — that it might help them focus and keep them on track.

Still, a large percentage of small business owners and salespeople — especially those already in business rather than just thinking about getting started — do not have a formal written business plan for their success.

Again, this does not mean that they have never thought about how they want to proceed or that they are running their business without any direction. It does mean that they have nothing written down that they can review and reference to guide their important business decisions.

It primarily means that they have never sat down and composed a plan.

There likely are many reasons that people in business have never written a plan, but few people are just outright opposed to having a written business plan.

It's not so much a case of indifference about whether they should have one or not or even rebellion against the idea. There are other issues in play.

Two Dozen Reasons To Procrastinate

There are many reasons, including some very personal ones, why people do not write a business plan.

Nevertheless, here are 24 (two-dozen) reasons that I have discovered over the years why people don't write a business plan, and there likely are many more:

- They don't know how to approach it,
- They are intimidated by the thought of doing it,
- They have never attempted one before,
- They don't understand what it should do,
- They aren't convinced of its value,
- They don't appreciate how it can provide benefits,
- They don't know what to include in it,
- They aren't sure what it should look like when it's done,
- They don't how many pages it should be,

- No one is requiring them to do it,
- No one will know if they have one or not,
- They aren't willing to set aside the time necessary to create it,
- They won't make the commitment to actually do it (it's not a high priority),
- They aren't willing or don't know how to create benchmarks to measure progress,
- They aren't sure how long of a term to use for the plan,
- They don't have a real vision for their business,
- They lack a clear mission,
- They have trouble defining specific goals for reaching the stated objectives,
- They have few, if any, functional systems in place,
- They lack strategic relationships or employees to work and accomplish the plan,
- They don't want to be held accountable to a plan,
- They are unable to project revenues or work output,
- They are unclear about their market, competition, or customers, and
- They don't treat what they have as a real business.

Feel free to add any additional reasons:

_____

_____

Not A High Priority

Writing a business plan is not something that is high on the "to do" list for existing small businesses, and it's easy to come up with an excuse or a stall for not getting started, not sticking with it, or not completing it.

On the other hand, a start-up business will often undertake one before launching to help them strategize their new venture or to seek investors.

This is particularly true when people have the time to invest in starting their business because they already have employment somewhere else and want their new venture to have a great chance for success.

Still, many businesses and businesspeople don't see a need for writing a business plan unless they need it to attract potential investors.

They figure that either they have a rough idea of what needs to be done, or they have survived this long without one so they might as well continue on this path.

There might be something to be said for just winging it and going with the flow as long as it works — but eventually something comes along that hadn't been considered or taken into account.

If nothing else, writing a business plan forces you to examine your marketplace, your product or service offerings, your pricing structure, how you spend your time, your revenue forecasts, your assets and resources, your competition, and other aspects of your business that you might not consider until forced to do so.

Rather than wait until unpleasant or unforeseen circumstances (including a market downturn or loss of market share) make you wish that you had taken the time to plan, why not put your ideas on paper now?

There's no time like the present to get started — regardless of how long you've been in business or how much revenue you have generated over the years.

It's A Personal Expression

Remember that a business plan — as we are discussing it here — is a guide for you. No one else has to see it.

You are not writing it for a letter grade like you would if you were in school. You are not trying to impress anyone. That's not necessary.

You may choose to share it — and it there are advantages to having all or parts of it seen by selected others — but you may choose to write it and keep it just to yourself.

It is a guide for your future.

It can be typed on the computer or written out longhand. The crucial part is the thought and the process that goes into preparing it.

The format and the actual way it looks when it is finished are not as important. It can be two pages or twenty pages — whatever it takes to address the key issues of your business success.

It's a personal expression of how you want to travel your success journey.

No two business plans are going to be the same — nor should they.

Write it for your needs alone.

3

What Does A Plan Look Like?

Getting A Feel For Your Plan

One of the reasons people don't write a business plan is because they don't know what it should look like when they are done with it — if they ever should attempt to do one.

Also, they don't know how much they should include in it.

They aren't sure what to include, what questions to answer, what its purpose is, or how many words or pages it should be.

Not having a good feel for what the business plan is all about or what it should do is probably why most business people (including salespeople) do not invest the effort in writing a plan.

People are constantly hearing or reading that they should write down their goals and plans, but they don't feel persuaded to do so.

They need a stronger reason to do this other than it works for other people who do it.

So let's approach it this way.

Writing a business plan forces you to consider elements that contribute to your success, challenges that you need to plan for and address, and a general scope of what you want to do. This is why the plan works.

It makes you focus and answer some very compelling questions.

That exercise in itself is quite powerful and will jumpstart your subconscious into pursuing your plan.

You're Not Writing A Book

The length of your plan isn't really the issue.

There are no requirements of length or any expectations — it just needs to be long enough to be useful and answer the questions you want to address.

A business plan such as we are talking about here is usually relatively short. For instance, a couple of pages could be sufficient. Then again, it might take 20 pages to do the job.

A lot depends on the nature of your business, the size of your organization, and how detailed and comprehensive you want to be in taking various factors into consideration.

Remember this is your document — prepared by and for you.

If your business consists of just you, and you offer a single product or service without much variation in pricing or margin — and you operate in a clearly defined geographic or demographic market — your plan can be very simple and brief.

However, as you have more products and services or product lines, that will be a factor because you'll want to address each one as a profit center.

Even if you are a consultant, designer, home stager, contractor, real estate sales professional, or other type of service professional, you may have different compensation plans and types of clients that you will want to address or allocate as they contribute to your general revenue, sales volume, and business success.

If you have a larger organization with various divisions, departments, or locations, your plan will necessarily be larger and more detailed to include each of them in your overall document.

Nevertheless, your plan just needs to be large enough to address the issues you want to include and nothing more.

Remember, you are the one who decides what to include and how many words to use to describe each topic.

Your plan doesn't need to look like anyone else's plan so don't worry about trying to compare it to another plan.

Before You Start Writing

Before, you sit down to write your plan, you're going to need to do some homework.

If you start writing your plan before having thought through the various components — including which ones to include in your document — you won't be able to get very far.

You don't need to address every question in your plan or necessarily include every section. However, you should at least ask yourself each question to determine if it's relevant to your business and if you can answer it. Then you decide whether to include it in your plan.

You won't be able to complete your plan until you supply the missing information.

In the following pages are the basic parts or categories of a business plan that you will want to address or include.

Some might be very brief. Some will be considerably longer.

Be as specific as you can — otherwise it's not the blueprint that you need but just some general ideas.

I have added a few blank lines after each section for you to make some notes of things that might come to mind as you are reading each topic.

This is not where you actually writing your plan, but it is where you begin taking notes of what you want to address and possibly include in your plan.

Then you can review your notes from this chapter and use them as a guide or template for completing your written plan.

History Of Your Business

What year did you begin your business, or when are you planning on a launch if this is a future endeavor?

_____

Why did you start your business, or why you join it if you are in sales or management of a larger organization and it's not your company?

_____

_____

_____

_____

_____

Where did you get the idea to start this business, or who or influenced you to begin?

_____

_____

_____

_____

_____

What types of clients have you served, do you intend to serve, or do you want to serve (businesses, consumers, any particular age group, professionals, government, private sector, just certain industries or demographics?

_____

_____

_____

_____

What products or services do you offer (or intend to provide), why did you select those and possibly not others, and how might that change in the future?

_____

_____

_____

_____

Have you or your company won any professional awards or honors for sales, community service, volunteer work, or offices held?

_____

_____

_____

_____

Do you have any particular bragging rights for the way you do business, a particular process or system you use or trademarked, something you invented or patented, a major contract you received, or market share?

_____

_____

_____

_____

_____

What geography do you serve or plan on serving (neighborhood, zip code, city or cities, county or counties or parishes, district, region, state or province, multi-state, national, international, or online)?

_____

_____

_____

_____

What type of business did you create or do you intend to have (sole proprietorship, partnership, LLP, LLC, PA, S-Corp, C-Corp)?

_____

What has been your general sales volume (dollars, units, or however you measure it) and general revenue history? For the past 10 years, 5 years, 12 months, and Y-T-D (year-to-date)?

_____

_____

_____

_____

What general challenges have you faced and how have you dealt with them in the past few years such as more direct local competition, online competition, economic slowdowns, cost increases for your materials, lower demand due to technology or sales lost to the competition, market saturation, or changes in consumer tastes and spending or buying patterns?

_____

_____

_____

_____

_____

_____

_____

Purpose Of Your Business

While you may have addressed some of this in thinking about or discussing the history of your business, you need to look specifically at your purpose — what you want to accomplish.

More than why you started your business, why you are associated with this particular business or company if you are in a sales or management capacity, what do you intend to accomplish, how do you plan on making people's lives better, and what excites you about running this business?

_____

_____

_____

_____

_____

_____

_____

What is or was not being addressed by existing businesses where you can gain customers and revenue?

_____

_____

_____

_____

_____

_____

Who benefits from what you provide, why you want to remain in business, and what makes your business special or unique?

_____

_____

_____

_____

What would your customers do for the products, services, or solutions you provide if you weren't in business?

_____

_____

_____

_____

_____

_____

Vision Of Your Business

Using the history and purpose of what you are doing (or what you are intending to do), formulate your big-picture vision (using as many words as necessary) of what you do and your general approach for continuing to stay in business and provide the kinds of products or services you offer as you appeal to your intended audience and maintain your market share or expand and create new markets.

Your actual statement (that you'll work on more in the next chapter) should be several sentences and address where you came from, where you are going, your awareness of market conditions and your ability to adapt, serving your core customer base, identifying new products or procedures for what you offer, your relative place in your industry, and other factors that indicate that you have really thought through and considered how you make a difference for the marketplace and the consumer. Just make some key notes here.

_____

_____

_____

_____

_____

_____

_____

_____

_____

_____

_____

_____

_____

Mission Of Your Business

Beginning with your vision, condense that into a very brief, actionable mission statement that is easy to remember, recite, and follow — to guide you, your staff, associates, and strategic partners in the delivery of what you offer.

Many people want to make this too long.

Chapter 5 will focus more on this, but it should be one sentence and fewer than 12 words — preferably fewer than 10. Make a few key notes here.

Use powerful words that include other words. For instance, to "deliver" or "create" a new kitchen requires that you assess, design, build, install, and achieve a finished kitchen. One word or action verb takes the place of several.

_____

_____

_____

_____

_____

_____

Core Values

As you are assembling your ideas of what you are as a business, including your purpose, vision, and mission, don't ignore or forget your core values and how they might apply or be incorporated into your business and your business dealings with the public, employees, trades, and other professionals.

Core values are those attributes or pursuits that define you as a person and therefore your business that cannot be set aside just to earn a buck. They guide your attitude, business ethics, and your decisions.

Honesty, integrity, compassion, resolve, persistence, perseverance, dedication, balance, resilience, fairness, preparation, diligence, commitment, honor, courage, leadership, fitness (mental and physical), and humility are such core values that might play a huge role in your business by defining how you relate to others and deliver your goods and services to the marketplace.

Note any from this list that apply to you:

_____

_____

_____

_____

_____

_____

_____

_____

Add any that you have that weren't mentioned:

_____

_____

_____

_____

_____

_____

Now, write down ones from the list (or not) that you want to embrace to provide direction for your business:

_____

_____

_____

_____

_____

_____

Be sure to include a complete spectrum of key characteristics that cover your life in personal, family, business, physical, mental, spiritual, and financial areas.

For instance, if family time is something you esteem, then you will want to make it is a priority in your schedule — to the extent possible (you still have to get some work done).

You'll also want to make sure that your employees or team members — and even key customers or clients — honor this as well, and you'll want to encourage them to observe this in their own lives and schedules if it's one of their core values.

If you feel that you need to close one or more days a week or allow your staff or associates time for religious observances, that is also part of your core values and should be so expressed.

If you think that community service or volunteerism is an important aspect of being a good corporate citizen or member of your area or neighborhood, factor that into your schedule and business plan. This would include serving on committees, attending meetings and events, and providing financial support.

As a part of who you are, you may decide to donate a portion of your receipts to a charitable effort that you believe in and support.

Physical fitness might be part of your core value system. If so, you will want to make time for biking, jogging, golf, tennis, or going to the gym — not as activities that you squeeze in or do because they are recreational, but as a valid part of building your business the same as other activities are, such as reading, research, prospecting, or sales.

The way you set and honor commitments with your staff, team members, trades, professionals, and your customers is part of your core value system. How you meet the expectations of your customers, employees, and associates and other key aspects of interpersonal relationships is something you should express.

Scheduling time for recharging your batteries is important for any leader, so express your intentions about time off, recreation, or breaks in activity.

Add in professional development time.

Keep things in balance so that one area does not monopolize your time or focus even though running and building your business is your main concern.

It's how you provide financially for you and your family, create employment for others (even if it's just trade partners or suppliers), and provide a valuable product or service to the marketplace.

Products/Services You Offer

What are the general products or services you currently offer (or which ones have you decided to offer if you are pre-launch currently) as well as the specific product names and their descriptions?

_____

_____

_____

_____

_____

_____

_____

_____

What are your current products or services designed to do, have they been independently tested or verified (including client or customer testimonials), and how do they align or compare with similar products or services on the market?

_____

_____

_____

_____

_____

_____

_____

Are you planning on adding any more, and if so, what will they do, and why do you think they are necessary or beneficial to the public and your business?

_____

_____

_____

_____

_____

What has been the general market acceptance of what you offer (or what do you anticipate it to be if you are a new business or planning on supplementing your line)?

_____

_____

_____

_____

_____

_____

How have you had to change what you offer as market
conditions, demand, sales pace, competition (including
those on the internet), government regulation,
licensing, new rules, or technology have impacted what
you offer or what people want?

_____

_____

_____

_____

_____

_____

What trademarks or proprietary claims do you have, or
can you make, and are there any unique or special
properties for what you offer?

_____

_____

_____

_____

_____

_____

Which products or services (if any) are in the works, which are being expanded or revised, which are ready for roll-out, which are being retired, and which are scheduled for review or updates?

_____
_____
_____
_____
_____

What is the projected timing for these reviews or product changes (including roll-out)?

_____
_____
_____
_____

How effectively are you reaching your target audience, and do you have any plans for maintaining or expanding market share?

_____
_____
_____
_____
_____
_____

What needs to be done to your products or services to keep them competitive (including sizes, models, styles, colors, features, options, and packaging) or to gain a larger share of the market?

_____
_____
_____
_____
_____
_____
_____

Is the gross margin or the markup on your products or services effective for maintaining or growing your business (including your wages, overhead, debt service, research and development, marketing, and profit)?

_____
_____
_____
_____
_____

Does your pricing structure need to be adjusted to be more competitive, to align more with national or online vendors, or to give you a greater rate-of-return?

_____
_____
_____
_____
_____

_____

_____

When would this need to happen, and what triggers would you look for?

_____

_____

_____

_____

How effective or efficient is your shipping, delivery, or installation system — including shipping costs; slippage; callbacks; returns; refunds; replacements for damaged, delayed, or defective shipments; transit time; and general customer satisfaction?

_____

_____

_____

_____

_____

_____

_____

_____

Geographic Markets You Serve

Once you identify the products, services, opportunities, or solutions you offer or intend to provide, look at the market areas you serve or desire to serve.

You briefly looked at this and addressed it in your history section. Here, you should expand your outlook about the markets you serve.

Do you have a neighborhood or small area focus where customers know who you are and come specifically to you by car, transit, or on foot; a drive-by location on a well-traveled street that anyone might visit (including people from outside your area); a location in a local or regional shopping mall; a destination site such as an entertainment venue or a resort; a citywide or area outlet or appeal; a regional location; a statewide or multi-state market; a national or nationwide scope; an international appeal or audience; an online or mail order presence to worldwide markets (solely or as part of a location based business); phone based (solely or in conjunction with other locations); or do you take your business to your customers at their homes or businesses, trade shows, expos, infomercials, webinars, or fairs?

Just where and how are you offering your products of services?

_____

_____

_____

_____

_____

_____

Consumers You Serve

Are you appealing to a particular gender, such as just men, just women, or primarily one sex or the other (allowing for gift shopping or generic or unisex items)?

_____

_____

_____

_____

Do you aim for the general populace or for general business customers to use your products and services?

_____

_____

_____

_____

_____

If you are marketing to consumers, are you focusing on a particular age group or segment of the population such as infants, toddlers, pre-school, elementary school, pre-teens, adolescents, teens, college-age, post-college, newlyweds, empty-nesters, 20s, 30s, 40s, 50s, 60s, seniors, retirees, elderly, or no particular age or group as long as there is a need for what you offer?

_____

_____

_____

_____

Do your customers (business or consumer) need or require any special skill, education level, knowledge, ability, life skills, experience, agility, coordination, or strength to use what you provide — or can anyone use it as long as they have a need and the ability to purchase it? Do they need to be a certain age?

_____
_____
_____
_____
_____
_____
_____

Are you primarily selling services or products to consumers ("B2C") in their homes, at a trade/home show, in your facility (sales center, office, retail location, kiosk, warehouse, or showroom), or virtually (by phone, mail, email, or infomercial), to other business ("B2B") at their place of business, at a home/trade show, special event, at your place of business (sales center, retail location, warehouse, or showroom), or virtually (by phone, mail, email, or infomercial) — or to a mixture of consumers and businesses? Do you see this continuing or changing in any way?

_____
_____
_____

_____

_____

_____

_____

_____

What percentage of your business comes from each source or venue?

_____

_____

_____

_____

_____

Are you targeting or appealing to specific income groups or sizes of businesses (or primarily going for mass market general appeal) because of the pricing structure of what you offer, the quality of your product, the life cycle of what you provide, the scope of your services, the number of similar or competitive products or services on the market, where you offer your items for sale, or where people may find them available?

_____

_____

_____

_____

_____

_____

_____

Define, as completely as possible, your ideal customer. When an opportunity presents itself or when a colleague approach you with a potential referral, you need to determine if this is a good fit for what you are doing and the direction you want to go.

Depending on whether you serve consumers or other businesses, your customer can be delineated in terms of where they live or operate their business, lifestyle or mission, family or company size, type of home or business they have, income or revenue range, number or layer of decision makers involved, amount of money they have to invest with you, and how quickly you can respond and complete the work or engagement.

_____

_____

_____

_____

_____

_____

_____

Your Objectives, Goals & Priorities

This is a tricky one because we tend to lump everything that we want to accomplish into the "goal" category when mostly they are objectives, and we don't distinguish between the relative importance of the various items (priorities).

So examine what you are doing and then answer what you want accomplish in terms of market areas or people served, products sold, new products or services developed or introduced into the market, market share, revenues, name recognition and visibility, branding, long-term impact, new technology, cutting-edge processes or products as protected through patents or trademarks, customer satisfaction, overall customer experience, vendor or trade partner relations, and other key areas of your business as expressed in broad concepts (**objectives**) and then with measurable specifics (**goals**) to attain those objectives — and which are the most important to tackle first and which are longer-term (**priorities**)?

Note how soon you want to achieve each of the various targeted items (immediately, 30 days, 90-days, 6 months, 1 year, 5 years)?

_____

_____

_____

_____

_____

_____

_____

_____

_____

_____

_____

_____

_____

_____

_____

_____

_____

_____

_____

_____

_____

_____

_____

_____

_____

Your Financial Position

This takes into account the history of your business in terms of annual billings, revenues, and sales — and it looks at future or projected sales. It also takes a look at your expenses and budget.

You don't have to include a budget or pro forma in your plan, but having one may help you evaluate your projected revenues and expenses.

What is your basic financial position as determined by cash-on-hand, bank deposits, stocks and other negotiable instruments, land and other assets, accounts receivable, leases, outstanding loans, debt service, recurring accounts payable (leases, rent, mortgages, licenses, taxes, utilities, phone), payroll, and similar expenses?

_____

_____

_____

_____

_____

_____

_____

_____

What are your projected revenues (daily, weekly, monthly, quarterly, or annually depending on the type and amount of business you have), and does your gross margin vary by the type of work you do?

_____

_____

_____

_____

_____

_____

How would changing prices (up or down to create a faster sales pace or more revenue per sale), doing

more sales, keeping more on each sale, or adding staff
change the financial picture of your business?

_____
_____
_____
_____
_____

What are your fixed and variable expenses?

_____
_____
_____
_____
_____
_____

Are any of these subject to change, or how could they
be changed to make you more profitable?

_____
_____
_____
_____
_____
_____

What building improvements, property/land, vehicles,
equipment, software, professional services contracts,
leases, or other long-term liabilities do you intend to
acquire or execute — and how will they help you run

your business more effectively, efficiently, or profitably?

_____

_____

_____

_____

_____

_____

_____

What types of financial assistance or capital (regardless of the source or the costs of that money) will you require, over what period of time, and how will you pay it back?

_____

_____

_____

_____

_____

_____

_____

_____

_____

_____

What are your sales goals and forecasts, what are your margins on various products and services, and what other sources of income (if any) do you have, such as royalties, rent, franchise fees, finder or referral fees, commissions, refunds, annuities, investments, or other residual payments?

_____

_____

_____

_____

_____

_____

_____

What are your financial requirements going forward, and can those be met through existing assets, current sales pace, projected sales activity, loans, grants, investments, going public, or other ways of supporting your operation — and what are your projected annual budgets (revenues and expenses) for the term of your plan?

_____

_____

_____

_____

_____

_____

_____

What type of financial record keeping are you using for bill paying, invoicing, receivables, statements, reports, and taxes? How is it done (you, your staff, outsourcing, paper system, or automated system), and how are you backing up your data?

_____

_____

_____

_____

_____

Is your current financial record keeping system satisfactory for you or do you think you might need to change something?

_____

_____

The Physical Part of Your Business

You looked at questions earlier in this chapter about how you serve your customer base from a geographic or locational standpoint. This section is similar but looks more at the physical requirements and characteristics of your business.

Do you have a location where customers and the general public can come to you, or do you operate out of your home (where people can visit you or just for you and your staff to have an office)?

_____

_____

_____

If you operate from your home, is it dedicated space such as a basement, home office, or garage (attached or detached), or is it space taken from the living room, dining room, or bedroom?

_____

_____

If this is the case, is this satisfactory for the near-term, or do you see making changes to the size and layout of your home office, or looking for office space away from home?

_____

_____

_____

Are you a free-standing store, showroom, or location that you lease or own where your consumers come to you, a leased or owned office or retail space in a building or shopping plaza with other stores of various types, an office you maintain but do not receive customers there because you sell at your customer's location or neutral sites (coffee shops, restaurants, hotel lobbies, shows, events), or an office where you conduct business primarily or entirely by phone or online rather than having consumers visit you?

_____

_____

_____

_____

Do you have a showroom or warehouse along with office space, or do you just maintain an office?

_____

_____

Do you maintain a single location or multiple sites, and are you planning on scaling back, maintaining, or expanding the number and type of locations?

_____

_____

_____

_____

_____

In addition to office space, do you think you might requires a warehouse, display center, showroom, retail space, call center, virtual offices, or other facilities to house your staff, showcase your products, receive your potential consumers, warehouse your machinery and inventory, allow for assembly or production, and store your vehicles and supplies — or can any of that be accomplished through remodeling of your existing space?

_____

_____

_____

_____

_____

Personnel Resources

Even if you are a sole proprietor or plan on starting your business that way, you likely do or will require and use the services of others in some capacity for sales, lead generation, marketing and promotion, production, administration, order fulfillment, delivery, installation, accounting, or market/product research.

You might have one or more partners or one or more employees (full or part-time). You might have paid or unpaid family members that work with you. Possibly you use seasonal workers or college interns also.

_____

_____

_____

_____

You could use independent commissioned salespeople, employment firms or agencies, trade contractors, professional services firms, consultants, virtual assistants, or collaborative strategic relationships to help you run your business.

_____

_____

_____

_____

_____

Determine how many people, in what general types of job descriptions, capacities, occupations, or skills, and what type of employment relationship is appropriate to help you sell, produce, and manage the work that you do (or intend to do). Which of them can bring in more business for you?

_____
_____
_____
_____
_____
_____
_____

How many people and in what general types of job descriptions, occupations, professions, or skills will you need to add, acquire, or create additional associations with as employees, virtual assistants, interns, independent contractors, professional services firms, or trade contractors to help you sell, produce, manage, deliver, install, and stand behind the work that you intend to do, and will you need to establish any new strategic relationships or identify other strategic partners to assist you in fulfilling your plan?

_____
_____
_____
_____
_____

_____

_____

What types of ongoing training programs, educational resources, seminars, workshops, and instructional materials do you have or use for new hires and existing staff to increase skill levels, proficiency, efficiency, and maintain overall competency?

_____

_____

_____

_____

What types of new training programs, materials, seminars, consultants, or other resources (including online) will you need to look for and get for new hires and existing staff to comply with federal or state regulations, increase skill levels, maintain competency, and gain a larger market share?

_____

_____

_____

_____

_____

Office Equipment & Systems

What types, amount, sizes, capacity, value, relative condition or age, and useable life of equipment and personal property do you have such as computers, file servers, telephone systems, audio-visual equipment, vehicles, presentation equipment, displays, furniture, security systems, tools, office supplies, file cabinets and storage units, books, manuals, software, spare parts, manufacturing lines, and machinery?

_____
_____
_____
_____
_____
_____
_____
_____

What other types, sizes, brands, styles, or capacities of furniture, storage, computers, machinery, software, and other types of office equipment or materials do you think you will require to execute your plan successfully — as new equipment or to replace aging or obsolete items?

_____
_____
_____
_____
_____
_____
_____
_____

In addition to accounting, payroll, and purchasing systems that you use, what have you developed or purchased to help you perform essential tasks such as recruiting, hiring, estimating, bidding, scheduling, record keeping, delivery, shipping, warranty, inspections, quality control, consumer relations, marketing, and sales?

_____

_____

_____

_____

_____

_____

_____

What other types of systems will you need to acquire, develop, have created, or use to carry out your plan — or replace systems, software, and equipment that are becoming obsolete or ending their useful life

_____

_____

_____

_____

_____

Inventory & Raw Materials On-Hand

How much finished product (if any) do you have on-hand for each model, size, and color you produce or offer for sale, how much of it do you have in various stages of completion, and what is the general condition, value, and age of your inventory?

_____

_____

_____

_____

_____

_____

Do they have an indefinite shelf life or are they perishable?

_____

_____

_____

How much finished product or partially completed product(s) will you need to have on-hand to fulfill the projected orders?

_____

_____

_____

What type of adjustment, expansion, or investment will be required to accomplish this — and can or should any of this be outsourced?

_____

_____

_____

_____

_____

How much time does an average order take to produce, complete, and deliver or install, what is your production capacity at any one time, and what would need to be done to increase or improve it?

_____

_____

_____

_____

_____

_____

Where do you obtain your raw materials for manufacturing or production (foreign or domestic sources, local or long-distance), how much do you have on-hand of the various types you use, and what is the general condition, value, and age of your materials?

_____

_____

_____

_____

_____

_____

Do any of your materials deteriorate over time, or are any considered to be hazardous or dangerous?

_____

_____

_____

_____

Branding And Marketing

What do you use or have in terms of general branding, logos, trademarks, service marks, brochures, site or vehicle signs, collateral materials, business cards, websites, blogs, social media profiles, point-of-sale displays, packaging, labeling, shipping materials, coupons, wall graphics, uniforms, and leave-behinds?

_____

_____

_____

_____

_____

_____

_____

What will you need to produce, purchase, supplement, add onto, or replace to promote your business to the marketplace and potential customers in terms of brochures, videos, automated presentations, kiosks, DVDs, site or vehicle signs, collateral materials, websites, blogs, social media profiles, wall graphics, uniforms, packaging, labeling, shipping materials, and leave-behinds?

_____

_____

_____

_____

_____

_____

_____

_____

What types or forms of marketing, promotion, and advertising are you currently using (print, electronic, signage, web, social media, referral, direct mail, agents, brokers, bird-dogs, events, shows, coupons, direct person-to-person, indirect word-of-mouth, infomercials, fairs, clinics, seminars, talk radio, interviews, open houses, or other types of outreach)?

_____

_____

_____

_____

_____

_____

Who is doing it (you, family member, an agency, a friend, staff, a marketing consultant, or it just happens with no one having specific responsibility for it)?

_____

_____

What are the results of those efforts in terms of effectiveness, volume of traffic, targeted leads as a percentage of overall response, overall costs, costs-per-lead, costs-per-sale, conversion rates of sales leads-to-appointments and appointments-to-a-sale, special events, incentive and coupon programs, and planned or anticipated campaigns for generating sufficient leads to make the sales and revenue goals of your plan?

_____

_____

_____

_____

_____

_____

_____

_____

_____

Sales Program

Any business needs to generate revenue to exist, and it takes sales to produce that revenue.

Currently how many people (employees, independent commissioned salespeople, strategic partners, online sales representative, or just you) are producing new sales leads, meeting or interacting with interested parties, selling your products and services, and following-up with them to retain them as satisfied customers and sources of referrals and repeat business?

_____

_____

_____

How might that need to change to accomplish your plan in terms of number of appointments set, general level of interest and ability to purchase of the leads that you see, chief objections raised, closing ratios, cancellation rates, conversion rates of appointments-to-sales, self-prospecting abilities and results, costs-per-sale, up-selling rates, average dollar volume-per-sale, amount of repeat customer sales and customer retention rates, and customer referrals — as well as the sales success of new products or services in current markets or new ones that you might be introducing to accomplish your business plan?

_____

_____

_____

_____

_____

_____

_____

_____

Business Model

This is a key facet of running your business well and making wise and effective decisions.

As you are looking at your markets, products, services, competition, margin, core values, and other key factors of your business, you need to determine what you do well, what you like to do, what has a great rate-of-return ("ROI" or return-on-investment), and who your ideal client or customer is to actually formulate a business model that defines what you do, where you do it, and who is the most likely to do business with you.

Anything not fitting that model can easily be ignored or not pursued in favor of looking for work that matches your model.

This is the best decision making tool that you can have for your business.

It can change over time as new opportunities, directions, and areas of expertise come along, but it still is going to accent your strengths — individually and as a company.

In Chapter 6, your business model will be addressed in more detail, but make some notes here about your ideal type of sale and size of the job (in terms of scope, scale, number of days to complete, revenue, or gross profit).

_____

_____

_____

_____

_____

_____

_____

_____

_____

_____

_____

Timetable For Your Plan

As you are thinking about and putting together your business plan, think about the period of time that it will cover.

Determine whether you are creating it for a few months with the idea of reassessing and possibly rewriting it at that time, or if you want it to serve as a plan for one calendar year and then be reissued for another year or replaced with another plan.

Maybe you want it to last for a few years, or for an even longer term.

Are you providing for periodic reviews and changes to your plan, is this one in a series of plans, and do you want to have an exit strategy written down (for the plan or your business)?

_____

_____

_____

_____

_____

_____

_____

Metrics & Benchmarks

To measure your progress and performance for what you are setting out to do, what types of gauges, tests, evaluations, surveys, and benchmarks are you building into your plan to use and monitor your effectiveness and keep you on track?

_____

_____

_____

How often do you intend to use them, and who is going to be tasked with doing them?

_____

_____

Which measures are going to be automated versus observations, consumer surveys, and other types of monitoring?

_____

_____

_____

_____

_____

Contingencies & Unknowns

You'll want to address the unknown and the unexpected.

What could happen to affect what you offer and your profit potential through market fluctuations, changing demand, economic conditions, technology, new or changing competition, shortages of materials, inflation, new taxes, new regulations or licenses, legal suits or challenges, possible product or service liability, excessive warranty claims, product recalls, defaults by customers and clients, cancelled orders, expensive repairs to machinery, downtime from storms or road or utility repairs affecting or disrupting access by the public, or losses not covered by insurance.

This doesn't need to be a crystal ball, just an expression that you are aware of issues that may present themselves.

_____

_____

_____

_____

_____

_____

_____

4

Beginning
With A Vision

Looking Ahead

One of the first steps in writing a business plan is to have a vision — a "big-picture" idea of what you are all about.

Look at what you want to accomplish, your commitment to success, what makes you different than similar companies or businesses, and why you think you will be successful. That will be your guide for your plan.

But, it's one thing to know that you need a vision to be successful, and another to create it. So, where do you begin?

How can you come up with a vision if you're not that sure about where you're going or where you want to be?

You need to examine your purpose and what you want to accomplish. If you haven't launched your business yet, figure out what you want to be.

If you're already in business but thinking of repositioning or reinventing yourself, it all starts with a vision.

"When I Grow Up"

All of us as children have had several episodes of dreaming about what we wanted to do when we grew up. Some were simple expressions like being a fireman, baseball player, nurse, doctor, or teacher.

However, many were visionary. That's what I'm talking about here.

Think back to how you planned in detail what would happen.

Maybe you were able to see it in pictures or even a video. Maybe you just saw it as a series of ideas or concepts.

Regardless, it's this type of comprehensive, unrestricted planning that is essential to creating a vision for your business.

What would the business of your dreams look like?

What product or service would you offer?

Would it be something you create or invent, or would it be something that already exists?

How would you be able to penetrate various markets and establish yourself and your business?

How you would make a name for yourself?

How would you be financially successful?

Having a business vision is very similar to the dreaming we did as a child or young adult.

We really need to "blue-sky" or let our minds run wild with all of the possibilities that could be.

Don't rule anything out unless it seems like something that you don't think you'd enjoy doing.

Then you start writing those down and organizing your thoughts. Your business plan is being born through your vision.

I'm giving you a few lines here and there throughout this chapter for you to make some notes as the ideas come to you.

Make use of them to capture your thoughts.

These notes are part of your vision.

You'll use them to create a more complete expression when you finish reading the entire chapter.

_____
_____
_____
_____
_____
_____

Making Sense of Your Vision

As you begin seeing parts of what you'd like to accomplish, you note them. Then you keep adding to them until a more complete picture emerges.

_____
_____
_____
_____
_____
_____

You may not see the whole thing as a movie. You may get it more in disjointed scenes. Then you'll have to connect it and make it flow.

Is your mental movie that you're watching making any sense to you?

_____

_____

Are you seeing what you want to accomplish? Any clue how you will adapt to changing market conditions and demand for your product or service?

How about obstacles or challenges you think you might have to meet or work around?

_____

_____

_____

How will you embrace technology in your business and make it work for you to facilitate production or marketing?

_____

_____

What type of help and resources (financial, raw materials, physical plant, marketing, sales, production, distribution, personnel, strategic relationships, referrals, systems) you will need to be successful? How can you describe your intentions in a meaningful way that will keep you excited make others want to pursue your vision with you?

_____

_____

_____

Forcing Yourself To Dream

Even if you are having trouble visualizing what form or shape your business should take, you must create a vision as a starting point for your success map.

If you can't see a scene unfolding in your mind or you don't think in word pictures, that's alright. There's another way to create a vision.

Imagine yourself to be a management consultant that is tasked with creating a vision for your company.

You look at your business as an interested outsider would and ask the same kinds of questions that will reveal what the vision actually is.

In this way you can learn what you want to do, why you feel it is worthwhile, what you are passionate about, and how to get started.

Then you can look at what you want to offer the public, what markets and demographics you want to serve, and what you think it will take to keep the business going and remain relevant in the marketplace.

Whether you actually visualize and see the concept of your business, or whether you have to approach it more objectively to get the answers you need, you still will have the essentials of your vision.

You will have created the big-picture.

A Vision Is Not Magnanimous

Your vision statement is not a magnanimous expression.

It is very personal. No one is judging you on your vision statement, and most people will never see it unless you choose to post it on your website or annual report.

Curing cancer or diabetes, saving the planet, and other such causes are not visions — not yours anyway unless your business is associated with such a large undertaking.

Even then, the larger objective likely would not be an appropriate vision for you without much more elaboration on how you saw that occurring.

Your vision needs to express in general terms what you intend to do, why you feel your business is necessary, how you intend to offer your products or services, who your customers are or will be, how you will grow your business or respond to changing market demand, and whether this is a relatively short-term or long-term proposition.

Remember this is a personal expression. It's your dream, your vision. You aren't doing this to impress anyone or win their approval.

It should not be based on what you think people would want you to believe in for your business but on what truly excites and motivates you.

Is It Really A Statement?

We call them vision statements — and they are — but the name is a little misleading.

When we hear the word "statement" we tend to think "sentence" or "short."

Vision statements — ones that are written correctly — are neither. They are statements in that they express your vision, but they typically run several paragraphs.

I'm not sure there is a better term for describing a vision other than statement, but it tends to connote something very brief rather than one more comprehensive.

Vision statements are long when compared to a mission statement, slogan, or tagline.

The vision should be expressed in several sentences and multiple paragraphs. It needs to tell your story.

Anything brief is not correctly describing the vision.

Conversely, the mission statement is a very brief synopsis of that — just a few words in one sentence.

A mission statement of more than one sentence is not proper either.

Jot down a few concepts here that you want to include:

_____

_____

_____

_____

_____

_____

_____

_____

_____

_____

_____

_____

_____

_____

Example Of A Vision Statement

Many companies confuse or mislabel their so-called mission statement when it really sets out their vision.

Some even have longer mission statements than vision statements — doing a disservice to both.

Since you likely have never written down your vision, let me give you an example of what one looks like.

We've all grabbed a cup of coffee, milkshake, burger, or other food items at a fast-food hamburger restaurant chain like a McDonald's so I think we can relate to it.

Here is a vision statement that I prepared for a fictional 24-hour hamburger fast-food restaurant that is relatively comprehensive:

We intend to be the restaurant of choice, or certainly in the running, 24-hours a day, whenever someone wants a good, quick, wholesome meal or snack, from breakfast, lunch, dinner, dessert, late night craving, or any time in between. Whether it is a full meal, something for the kids, a soft drink, coffee, ice cream, dessert, salad, or a sandwich, we need to be ready to meet those food and beverage needs of people within our market reach.

As market conditions permit, we will expand the number of our locations and our menu offerings so that we can be available and responsive to more and more people as well as our core customers.

While we realize that there are other food and dining choices available for people, including higher-end restaurants and dining at home, we encourage people to choose us as often as they can and remain up to the challenge of meeting the demands of serving a consistently tasty meal, snack, or beverage at any time of the day or night.

To insure that people keep returning day-after-day, and time-after-time, we commit to offering a fresh, clean, safe, and friendly environment with professional service and only the finest, freshest ingredients that we can obtain to offer a uniformly good product at a reasonable price.

We welcome and accommodate people of any age and ability, from infants to the oldest among us, including business meetings, families, sports teams, friends, birthday parties, celebrations, and casual get-togethers.

The Vision Expresses the Ideal

Notice how much information is embodied in a vision statement such as this one — and that it's not packed with a bunch of flowery words.

It acknowledges what they are as a company and discusses or takes into account their purpose, direction, competition, market share, growth, quality of product and service, consistency, customer appeal, the customer experience, repeat visits, word-of-mouth marketing, and target audience.

However, it does not offer details or specifics on how everything is to be done.

It's enough just to express what you want to do and the impact you want to make.

In essence, it is the vision of your ideal business — what you really would like to be able to achieve as a business.

It doesn't mean that all of this is happening right now, but that is the vision for what you want your business to be.

It is comprehensive in a general sort of way.

It doesn't say how things are going to be done in terms of specifics, but it lays out the current business model and future intentions.

This would be what you want to do and why you are in business.

This is what your vision needs to do.

Once written, insert it into your plan.

5

Condensing It To A Mission

Mission Statements Are Brief

While vision statements are long, mission statements are brief — the shorter the better.

Some companies miss the point and try to make them too long and complicated. In fact, some companies have longer mission statements than vision statements.

This is fundamentally wrong. The vision needs to actually express what and how you are going to do something.

While landing on the moon for NASA, doing kitchen or bath remodels, or being known for a particular product or service may factor into a vision statement, they are not sufficient to create the total business concept.

The vision statement needs to describe the nature of the business in terms that create some enthusiasm for being in that particular business.

Then, the mission statement comes behind that to provide specifics to the vision statement and give the business direction — in the fewest words possible.

They need to be short enough for everyone — employees, trade contractors, and strategic partners — to remember and even recite.

This way, the mission statement will be the powerful guide to behavior, action, and performance that it needs to be.

I like to see mission statements limited to no more than 12 words, and fewer than 10 is even better. It must be just one sentence.

It may take some work to cut it back to this length, but this is what an effective mission statement will be.

Jot down a few words or phrases that might express your mission. Don't worry about the length at this point:

_____

_____

_____

_____

_____

Mission Statements Are Not Slogans

Be careful in making your mission statement short and to the point that you are not creating a slogan or tagline.

You are not trying to create a marketing message for public consumption. Instead, you need to be revealing what your daily actions should be to carry out your vision and make it a reality.

While vision statements are necessarily general in nature, the mission statement is very specific.

It states in the fewest words possible what every team member needs to do and focus on at all times throughout the day to keep the business on track.

There is no ambiguity or room for interpretation in a mission statement. It translates the vision into action and gives it momentum.

It delivers the vision to the public by instilling in the team the minimum level of acceptable conduct for the business.

Example Of A Mission Statement

Using the example I provided in the last chapter for the vision of the fictional hamburger restaurant, the following are some possible mission statements that express that vision of that restaurant experience in much the same way as you might create the one for your business — from one that is a good first draft or attempt to the shortest it can be and still be effective.

This first one is 32 words. It expresses the vision and is a good first attempt at the mission.

It is too long, however:

> *To offer a reasonably priced, consistently good meal and dining experience each time a customer visits us that makes them happy they dined with us and looking forward to their next visit.*

This next one at 20 words is quite a bit shorter but not definitive enough because it could apply to most any restaurant and not just the fast food hamburger restaurant that we are describing:

> *To offer a good dining experience at an affordable price to make sure customers want to return again and again.*

This next one is half the length of the first one at just 16 words and makes a good statement, but it still lacks the fast food part of the equation:

> *To be the restaurant of choice for good, quick, affordable food that keeps people coming back.*

This last statement captures the mission in the fewest words possible at only 9 words and leaves no doubt that this is a fast food dining experience rather than other types of dining.

Leaving out any of the words would change the mission:

To provide a consistently good, fast food restaurant experience.

Keeping Just The Important Words

All 9 words in this example are important.

It's possible to shorten this final mission statement to 7 words by taking out the words "fast food" but then it would be competing with all restaurants and would be like the earlier, more wordy attempts.

The phrase "fast food" is necessary because it defines and delineates the scope, mission, direction, and focus of this restaurant that is only interested in being the best fast food restaurant available — and not any other kind of restaurant.

The word "To" at the beginning of the statement might seem unimportant, but it creates the charge.

This is something that everyone strives for and wants to do. It doesn't exist or happen without effort and commitment.

Marching Orders

Notice that the words in the mission statement give everyone their performance guidelines for the business — otherwise referred to as "marching orders."

The quality, temperature, and appearance of the food; the speed with which it is delivered; the accuracy of the order; the attitude, friendliness, and appearance of the employees; and the cleanliness and appearance of the facility (including the tables, windows, service area, kitchen, condiment area, restrooms, and floors) are all addressed in this simple statement.

This is the type of mission statement you are seeking — the briefest one possible that sets out exactly what you want to do and can be remembered and recited by all of your team members, including employees, contractors, associates, and strategic partners.

You want a mission statement that clarifies the vision in the fewest words possible.

Think of some key points you want to include in your mission statement to provide direction to your team:

_____

_____

_____

_____

_____

Using Powerful Words

To create a mission statement using the fewest words possible, look for powerful words that convey the meaning of several other words.

For instance, you can say that you want to build "quality" or create "value." You also can just state that you offer or are committed to building the "best" or something similar that would include the other terms without specifically mentioning them.

Using the word "offer" or "provide" takes into account many other words and concepts, such "design," "build," "create," "produce," and "deliver." They are included.

Therefore, look for ways that you can eliminate words and replace them with a stronger, more inclusive word.

Use as many different words as you like in your vision statement, but keep them to a minimum in your mission statement.

Here are 12 lines — the maximum number of words you should have (strive for fewer).

Put one word one each line until you have the fewest number of words that you are happy with to express your mission. You can erase or line through words that you decide not to use.

Then you will have a mission statement:

1 _____

2 _____

3 _____

4 _____

5 _____

6 _____

7 _____

8 _____

9 _____

10 _____

11 _____

12 _____

Make sure that there are no extra words — words that could be removed without changing any meaning or sentiment.

Now you can insert this into your plan.

6

Determining A Business Model

The Heart Of The Plan

As I talked about in Chapter 3, the business model is a fantastic decision-making tool for your business. It makes a great component of your business plan. In fact it is the core of your plan.

Some companies and businesses have an informal business model without a formal business plan, and they use it to make decisions.

However, when properly constituted, the business model is part of and an expression of the business plan. It is slow to change or be amended.

The business model tells everyone with whom it is shared what the basic nature is of the company, the general mission of the company (actual mission statement or a paraphrase), types and locations of clients or customers that are to be served, the nature of typical needs that people have who are to be served, the scope or scale of a typical project or engagement, the average price or price range of a typical order or project, and the marketing effort that typically is used to reach and attract the target segment.

Colleagues who want to help you will often approach you and ask what an ideal referral is for you so they can look out for potential business and send it your way when there is a good match.

You will answer their question about the type of customer that is both best for you and the most enjoyable to work with from the information contained in your business model.

You won't have to think about it. It will be something you can readily share.

The Model Expresses The Plan

There is no formal template or guideline for preparing a business model. It can be a sentence or two or a few paragraphs.

However, it should be something that once thought out and conceived can be taught throughout your company or business to everyone that interacts with the public on behalf of the business so that promises aren't made and customers aren't pursued that are outside the business model — unless there is a very good reason that you or other decision-makers determine.

Occasionally you might determine that a particular job, customer, direction, or client is prestigious or important enough in terms of visibility or testimonial value that a job will be bid on or undertaken that is outside the scope of your business model.

This would be handled on a case-by-case basis. If too many of these are considered and pursued, then the business model probably needs to be revisited to determine if it really expresses the needs and desires of your business.

Similarly, a job or project may be considered because you want to gain some particular expertise by working on it.

Essentially, however, your business model frames the type and scope of the work you do.

Determining Your Business Model

To create your business model, begin with what you are really good at — whatever skill, talent, knowledge, or expertise that this might be — and what you really enjoy doing. Chances are good that most of your work falls into these areas already.

_____

_____

_____

_____

_____

_____

Then you need to quantify it.

Determine what your ideal job or project is in terms of target audience that would engage your services or purchase from you, the optimal size or scale of the job (physically or financially) that you like to work with, the preferred price point or range, and the desired time to complete the job, project, or order.

_____

_____

_____

_____

_____

You may define your business model as just working with a certain size business in terms of their revenue, volume, or production — or a consumer of a certain geographic location, income range, needs, requirements, size or characteristics of their residence, or lifestyle.

_____

_____

_____

_____

If you are a "B2B" company where you provide products and services to other businesses or businesspeople, you can frame your model in terms of the likely decision-making process in your potential customers and clients.

For instance, you may focus on public companies or private ones, ones with a board of directors or not, a company where the owner makes the decisions and you have access to that person, one where the vice president or department head can make a decision without sending it up through the channels, one where any purchasing decision has to reviewed at multiple levels, or one where everything has to have 3 or more bids before a decision can be reached.

_____

_____

_____

Maybe you only offer products in certain sizes, colors, or markets. Maybe you only serve certain demographics.

_____

_____

_____

_____

_____

You might find that you are comfortable with a certain size job, scope, or project (less than $2,500, around $5,000, $5,000-10,000, $10,000-$15,000, over $50,000 or any other range or price point) or a certain size order (100 pieces, 1,000, 5,000, 50,000, or whatever quantity works for you).

_____

_____

_____

_____

_____

You are able to fulfill this request very effectively and efficiently because you are very good at it and really enjoy doing it plus your resources are optimized working with this type of a job or order.

If this is the case, then this would form the basis of your business model — and you would jump at any request matching this scenario because it would coincide with your business model.

Just as scale models of cars, bridges, or buildings resemble or reflect what the full-size version of that object will be when fully developed, your business model similarly captures the essence of what your business is all about and how it will be comprised if it can mirror or replicate the model.

Making Decisions With Your Model

When you consider bidding on or accepting a job or order that is substantially above or below the range expressed in your business model, your first inclination might be to get it or do it anyway for the revenue and the business.

However, you likely would, and should, reject it as not fitting your business model and being outside your comfort zone — unless you have strategic relationships with other companies or individuals who can undertake such a job on a referral basis from you.

The decision would not be based so much on whether you could do the work but on the fact that it's just not a good use of your time and resources.

In the case of a job bigger than or more complex than what you normally do, it might require more labor or a different set of performance and completion standards than you are accustomed to doing.

In terms of something smaller, it might tie up your resources for a smaller than desired financial return while you miss out on being available to do work that is consistent with your model.

Whatever your business model states, a proposed or potential assignment or order will coincide and fit within the parameters of your model or it won't. You are interested in a good fit and not as much, or not at all, in things that don't.

Of course, cash flow, location of the job, the amount of other work you have at the time, whether this is a client or type of work that you want to acquire regardless of the size of the bid or order, whether you have done work for this customer or client before, and whether you want to gain experience with a job or order of this nature all factor into whether you are interested in the job.

Nevertheless, with all other factors being equal, you would normally reject a job not coinciding with your business model to allow you the time and energy to pursue jobs that fall within the scope of your model.

You certainly don't want to take on work that you normally don't do and risk being too busy with it that you have to pass up a job that is better suited for you.

Therefore, your marketing and your sales efforts would be directed toward generating interest and making sales with people or businesses in your target audience — as defined by your business model.

7

Setting Goals

Starting With Your Objectives

There's a lot of emphasis on goal-setting, but most of it is misdirected. What commonly are labeled as goals actually are not goals at all. Rather they are objectives or targets.

This is such a common misconception.

So, before you can set goals, you have to have at least one objective — something you want to attain. You can't just have a goal by itself. You have to be aiming for a greater attainment.

Even if you said you wanted to lose 8 pounds (or weigh 8 pounds less than you do now or attain a certain weight in pounds) by a certain date, you wouldn't just choose this for no reason.

It would necessarily factor into a larger plan.

Maybe you have a reunion, graduation, or wedding to attend and you need to fit into an outfit you already own or one you purchased for the event.

Perhaps you want your clothes to fit better, to wear something you have that currently doesn't fit, to be healthier, to match a weight you had previously, to win a friendly competition or race you are having with someone else to accomplish this first, or to set an example for your family or friends.

Maybe you are doing a photo shoot or video where you want to look a little thinner than you do now.

Whatever the reason, losing the weight is the objective. How you go about it, how rapidly you do it, how you measure your progress and success, and the methods you choose can all be part of your goals and strategies.

So what is the overall accomplishment or objective you are trying to achieve?

It could be many things, but once you determine that, you can establish goals that will help get you there.

For instance, losing weight, having a larger savings account, making money in the stock market, completing a marathon, winning a sales contest, and other such undertakings or plans are objectives.

They set out an overall picture or desire but don't specify how or when it is to happen (unless a fixed date is part of the objective) and how you will know if you have done enough to accomplish your original objective.

Determining Your Objectives

You must determine and then enumerate specific objectives that you want to accomplish as part of your business plan.

Having a financial "goal" is actually an objective.

It might be a specific number, but it's a general statement for the direction of your business.

Again, many statements which are passed off as goals are actually objectives. Whether it's winning a gold medal at the Olympics, breaking 80 on the golf course (or perhaps 70), winning a sales contest, landing a specific account, or just doing better than last year, these all are objectives.

Other objectives would be attaining a larger market share, introducing a new product or service, opening up a new market, building a new plant or office, relocating to more visible space, appealing to a new demographic, expanding your business, franchising your business, changing or expanding your delivery system, increasing your revenues, getting web traffic, creating e-commerce, or going public.

_____

_____

_____

_____

_____

_____

_____

_____

Objectives need goals to help them happen, and then goals need action plans.

No one sets out to accomplish the entire objective all at once because it must be defined, quantified, and broken up into achievable goals that will add up to accomplishment of the objective.

You can't graduate from college as a freshman on the first day of class. You have to have strategies and goals for completing each class successfully (required ones and electives) and make consistent progress toward the larger objective of a college degree.

Creating Priorities

If you have several objectives, you will need to prioritize them in terms of which are the most important to achieve, which will offer the greatest return, which will be the easiest or quickest to accomplish, or which will be the most satisfying for you to complete — whatever means the most to you in terms of how you want to tackle your objectives.

Priorities determine where you will focus and devote your time, and they can shift depending on what is the most important to you at any given moment.

Even though something may seem relatively minor when compared to other more pressing or comprehensive issues or tasks, you may decide that it is relatively simple or easy to accomplish so you devote a few hours to it and complete it.

While it didn't have a high priority until that moment, when you decide to work on it and finish it, you have made it a top priority.

Once completed, you can go back to your normal priorities.

Normally, your priorities establish the important tasks in the order they will be tackled. Often, they are the most difficult or time consuming to do.

Occasionally, a simple task can be elevated to a top priority for the sake of completing it and crossing it off the list.

Establishing Your Goals

To reach your objectives, you will need to complete a series of goals successfully. Your goals are measurable and achievable statements that break the objectives up into several parts.

If you want to introduce a new product or achieve a certain revenue target, you don't set a date on the calendar and just roll it out or check your ledger on that date without a lot of other tasks being accomplished in the interim.

_____

_____

_____

_____

There must be a series of parallel or consecutive steps that build upon each other to bring you closer and closer to achieving your particular objective as they are completed successfully.

Essentially, goals exist at four different levels — immediate, short-term, intermediate, and long-term — and help accomplish your objectives in stages or parts.

The four stages of goals are not rigid as to the time or activities they encompass — just in their degree of immediacy and focus.

Immediate Goals

Immediate goals are the shortest-term goals that exist. They also are very specific and leave no doubt as to what you need to do to accomplish them — and the date or time by which they are to be done.

Time is of the essence in completing these goals.

Depending on what you want and need to accomplish, they can be as short as an hour, a few hours, a workday, or somewhat longer, such as a 48-hours, 72-hours, a week, 10-days, 2-weeks, or a month (30-days). Because they are very short-term in nature, you will only have one or two that you are pursuing at any given time.

These necessarily are high-priority goals.

_____

_____

_____

_____

_____

Your immediate goals will specify the timing for completion (certainly to the day and possibly even to the hour) and the actual work product or item to be produced (submitting a proposal, mailing a letter, completing or delivering a report, filing a document with an official agency, applying for funding, producing a campaign, filling a position).

It will also tell you how to recognize that you are done.

Because of the immediacy of these goals, you should focus on them intently to complete them within the time frame you have given yourself.

In some cases the deadlines will be established for you (such as a submitting a proposal, bid, or request for funding), and in others they will be self-imposed (something you desire to complete by a certain time).

Either way, you can monitor your progress and know very soon if you are on target, if you are likely to be successful in meeting your goal, or if you need to evaluate your schedule and possibly modify your goals or expectations.

Short-Term Goals

Short-term goals are the next shortest goal terms but longer than immediate ones.

Some people choose not to even use the immediate goals and just use short-term and long-term goals.

However, that doesn't allow for immediate activities or for as many benchmarks and opportunities over time to monitor your progress and adjust your course as necessary for your success.

Depending on what you want and need to accomplish, short-term goals take over after immediate ones. The duration can be days, weeks, months, or up to a year or a little longer.

Remember, these are your definitions, and short-term goals require consistent focus and effort though not as constant as the immediate ones.

_____

_____

_____

_____

_____

The potential trap with short-term goals is procrastination or putting off working on them because they aren't immediate.

Intermediate Goals

Intermediate goals are the in-between goals. They are longer-term goals than short-term but not completely long-term ones.

They take into account projects and tasks that need more time to accomplish than what would typically be thought of as short-term so they fall into the intermediate goals category.

Intermediate goals generally have time windows of several months to a year or two.

Again, the actual definition of the time they cover and the type of work that these goals would encompass are entirely up to you.

_____

_____

_____

_____

Intermediate goals will not require constant focus, but progress on them will need to be regularly monitored.

Long-Term Goals

Long-term goals are the longest-term goals.

They can run from 2-5 years, and perhaps longer.

Again, the definition of the timing and what constitutes a long-term goal are entirely up to you.

These activities will receive your attention, and you will want to monitor their progress but in a manner appropriate for the length of time to complete.

Over time, parts of these goals may gain higher urgency or priority and have aspects of them assigned shorter-term goals.

_____

_____

_____

_____

They could possibly be redefined or eliminated depending upon such factors as market conditions, demand for your product or service, a new direction you decide to take, and how other goals have been completed.

Goals Provide Focus

Remember that your goals exist to give you day-to-day focus on your objectives and keep them in sight.

You should measure and monitor progress on your goals and make changes in your schedule and expectations accordingly.

The measurements don't have to be anything elaborate, and you will know if extenuating circumstances have thrown off your schedule.

Nevertheless, it's easy to look at sales numbers, revenue, margins, variance from budget, and other specific numbers or ratios — as well as key economic indicators that may impact your business — to see how you measure up to your goals.

_____

_____

_____

_____

Your goals also are subject to moving between categories as market conditions or your priorities change.

Short-term goals can take on a higher priority and move to immediate. They also can lose urgency and move back to intermediate.

The same type of movement can occur among the other categories as well.

8

Writing Your Plan

This Is Your Personal Plan

Remember that your business plan is a document for you and your business that is written by you. It doesn't need to please, or be approved by, anyone else.

You aren't going to publish your plan anywhere, and few people will see your entire plan. That is entirely up to you.

It must be personal for it to be the guide that you need it to be.

This is your success journey that you are planning and mapping. Your employees and strategic partners are welcome to take the journey with you, but you must be the guide. Your plan will be your GPS for your journey.

You can request and receive the assistance of others in your company, strategic partners, consultants, family, or friends — or you can write it entirely by yourself.

Ultimately it is your content. Therefore, you need to be the one to write it.

You Must Actually Write It

When you actually make the commitment to have a business plan, and whatever format it might take when it's completed, one thing is certain — it won't do you any good as a planning tool until it is actually written.

Whether you write it entirely by yourself or you have help putting it together, it still has to be created on paper.

Notice that there are no templates in this book with "fill-in-the-blanks" to provide much of the text already written and asking you just to supply some key dates, numbers, names, and specific aspects of your business.

You can go that route, but a template approach takes your personality out of the document.

You need to have a document that serves you because it expresses what you want it to say. It shouldn't be a document largely written by someone else (a software developer) with just a few items supplied by you.

Your business plan should be written in your own words to convey what you want it to — long or short, detailed or fairly simple.

Remember that your business plan is a guide to help keep you on track, help you define your goals and strategies, establish what you want to attain in terms of market share and revenue, and allow others to participate and sign on to your plan as you share aspects of it with them.

It is not a solicitation for investors.

Include whatever items from Chapter 3 that you feel will help tell your story, guide your performance, motivate you and your team to accomplish your goals, provide direction for your team, and serve as a solid map for your future — for the length of time you designate for the plan.

Then write it out.

Organizing Your Ideas

There are a couple of ways you can approach creating your written plan.

You can make an outline from the suggestions I gave you in Chapter 3. Then you can use the notes that you made in that chapter to begin creating a more complete text that will answer the questions and make sense to you as a road map for your success journey.

You also can approach writing your plan as if you are telling a story.

Answer the questions and address the major points of Chapter 3, but treat it more like you are have a conversation with a very close friend.

Tell your friend on paper all of the details on why you started your business, why you think it will be successful, why you think there is a need for what you provide, the type and amount of help you're going to need at various stages of your journey, the challenges you likely will face along the way, and how you will know at various points whether you are on target or not.

You Can Make Changes

Your business plan doesn't have to be perfect. Don't think that you can't even begin your plan because you don't want to mess it up or that you can't do it justice. It is, after all, your private and personal plan.

There can be a typo or scratch out or two. It can have imperfect grammar. It's the content that's important.

No one is going to be judging you on how well you put it together or addressed the various aspects of your business.

No one is going to critique how you wrote it — unless you share your plan and invite people to comment on what you have written.

You just need to create something.

You can tweak or change your plan as you go along, but without a written plan at the outset, you have nothing to guide you and nothing by which to measure your progress.

Without an initial written plan, there is nothing by which to compare your progress, measure results, or update your plan.

Spending Time With Your Plan

Your business plan will help you make decisions and avoid expensive missteps or mental back-and-forth discussions with yourself about whether to bid on a project or go in a certain direction. You will have already considered that and addressed it in creating your business model.

As a result of having a written business plan — as opposed to having no formal or specific plan at all or just a general idea of what you want to do in your mind — there will be no more relying on just your memory for what you want to do. It will be written out.

You will be less likely to vary from your plan or intentions this way and will be much better equipped to focus on what you want to accomplish.

You will be able to direct your money resources, time, and energy in a much more focused way.

Also, the more time you spend with your plan reviewing it and committing it to memory (not so you can recite it to anyone but just that you know it very well), the more forceful and effective you will become.

You will be internalizing the efforts and results of your planning, and that will provide subconscious support for your decisions and actions.

9

Sharing Your Plan

Getting Input From Others

Your business plan is a document for you and your business that is written by you.

It doesn't need to please anyone else.

Therefore, it doesn't need to receive the approval, agreement, consensus, input, or consent of anyone else before you complete it and put it into motion.

However, as I mentioned in the previous chapter, you may want to request the assistance of others to help you write your plan and pull your thoughts together — people in your company, strategic partners, consultants, family, friends, mentors, or trusted advisors.

While seeking the input of others is not a requirement in putting your plan together, it might be very beneficial.

This would be especially true if you are a start-up business that wants to hit the ground with some initial momentum, if you are expanding your business, or if you are attempting to assert yourself in a very competitive marketplace.

Sharing your plan or your intentions with anyone at any phase of the process is not required. Nevertheless, it may be desirable to do it in three different ways, and it is important that you to do in one specific additional way.

Three Ways To Share Your Plan

You may share your plan — while you are writing it to get ideas and concepts, or after you are finished it (with either a section of it or the entire plan) for any details you might want to include that were overlooked.

However, there are three options or alternatives that you have to involve others in what you have prepared.

First, you may share the *entire plan* with your employees or team, your mastermind group, your mentor, or anyone else that you can trust to have your best interests in mind and will respect the contents of your plan.

Anyone who is going to try to sabotage the plan or otherwise belittle it should not be involved — and you may rightly question keeping them on your team.

Second, you may choose to share just <u>*certain parts*</u> of your plan with certain groups of people.

You can show everyone the same few parts or be selective in which group gets to comment on various parts or sections of your plan, such your mission, vision, objectives, goals, and resources.

Third, you can refer to <u>*key parts*</u> of your plan without mentioning that they are part of your plan.

On your website or blog, you can publish your mission if you like. You can talk about your business model (without directly calling it that) by describing your ideal client or referral, your products or services, and your preferred or intended markets.

You also can put various parts of this in your social media profiles and your 30-second commercial.

Again, you can do as much or as little of this as you choose; however, I think that promoting your general business model online and in your advertising will help generate the type of business you are looking for the most.

Publishing Your Mission Statement

Get as much or as little input from others as you think you need to craft your business plan effectively. Share it with others in ways you feel are appropriate.

Then, the *one thing* you need to publish and promulgate regardless of whether you share any of the rest of your plan is your mission statement.

It doesn't have to published on your website or social media profiles specifically as your mission statement, but the concept needs to be shared with those who can help you fulfill it.

You want all of your staff, trade partners, strategic relationships, and contractors to know and understand your mission completely so that it will guide their performance and help you deliver to the public what you are committed to doing.

10

Using Your Plan

It's A Tool To Be Used

Your business plan is a tool — the same way a hammer, saw, screwdriver, drill, measuring tape, square, computer, calculator, brochure, website, business cards, and pen or pencil are all tools for your business.

It won't do you any good unless you create it.

It's OK initially to have a business plan that you carry around in your head, but you'll want to find the time to actually put it on paper.

This will help you crystallize your thinking, determine if you have addressed all of the important details, show you where you may have overlooked something or not thought it through as well as you could have, and give you a solid plan for making decisions and attracting strategic partners, employees, and resources as you move forward.

It will help you seek the business that you are the most qualified to handle and help you be a more viable and efficient business.

It will help you compete effectively in your marketplace and get the business that you deserve to undertake.

However, your business plan won't do you any good unless it really guides you. It can't just be a document that sits on the shelf or lives in your desk drawer.

Therefore, you need to read it, internalize what it contains (after all you are the one who wrote it), and memorize what's in (not to recite it but to be extremely familiar with it so that it guides your actions effortlessly).

It won't do you any good unless you use it and allow it to be the blueprint you intended it to be when you created it.

Your plan is designed to serve as your official guide and layout for your business. It will show you how to get where you want to go — using the information you have put into it.

Your vision, mission, objectives, priorities, goals, business model, resources that you have on hand as well those you require for the future, projected revenues and margins, marketing program, sales targets, and ultimately a budget that stems from this will make you a formidable business that knows where it is going and how to get there.

Planning Is Vital

Don't skimp on the planning or begrudge the time that may be required to do a good job.

You will only be hurting yourself.

Take the time necessary to examine all aspects and areas of your business.

Go back through the questions I gave you in Chapter 3 and use the blank lines to jot down some notes and ideas.

Then assemble your thoughts and write it down.

Now you'll have a plan that you can run with. You can modify it as you go along, but you need to at least create something.

This doesn't have to be completed in a single session or over a weekend.

There's no deadline for completing your plan, but it's not as hard as you may have thought before reading what I have given you. The sooner you have a written document, the sooner it can begin focusing your thinking toward accomplishing what you have defined.

Now, It's Up To You

This is your document so you don't need to check with anyone else before getting started. You don't need to review what other businesses have prepared or go online to find a template.

Simply write your story.

Approach it with the future in mind. Where do you want to be when you get there? Let your plan be your map for guiding you to that point.

If you need help in conceiving, drafting, creating, formulating, or writing your business plan – or you need someone to discuss it with as you are preparing it, contact me. I am a resource for you.

Have fun examining what you want to do and then committing it to paper.

Good luck structuring and using your plan.

Steve Hoffacker

Steve Hoffacker, AICP, CAASH, CAPS, CGA, CGP, CMP, CSP, MCSP, MIRM, is principal of Hoffacker Associates LLC, a new home sales training and real estate coaching company based in West Palm Beach, Florida.

Steve is an award-winning new home sales trainer and coach, commercial real estate broker, marketing consultant, award-winning photographer, best-selling author, blogger, teacher, and salesman.

For more than 30 years, he has helped homebuilders, new home salespeople, Realtors®, small business owners, and other professional salespeople to be more visible, competitive, profitable, and effective — and to really enjoy themselves as they pursue their business.

He has embraced the concept of universal design as an effective strategy for delivery aging-in-place solutions for people wanting to remain in their homes for as long as they choose. He has written books on this subject.

As many of you are entering this aging-in-place field and developing a business plan to accommodate your new career path and business direction, this book will be a great resource for you.

Regardless of the type of business you have, many of the suggestions and ideas Steve provides in this book are a new interpretation of common business planning strategies. Use them for your success.

www.ingramcontent.com/pod-product-compliance
Lightning Source LLC
Chambersburg PA
CBHW032331210326
41518CB00041B/2071